5/14

W9-BTZ-588

CHEMICAL ENGINEERING
AND Chain Reactions

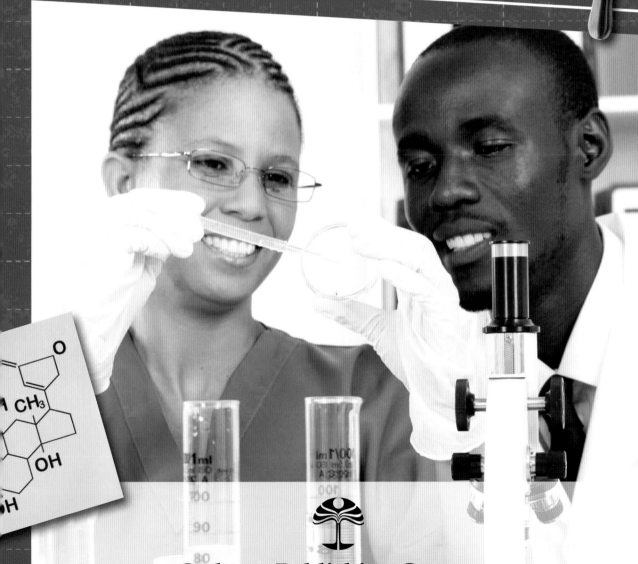

Crabtree Publishing Company
www.crabtreebooks.com

Robert Snedden

Crabtree Publishing Company

www.crabtreebooks.com

Author: Robert Snedden
Publishing plan research and development:
    Reagan Miller
Project coordinator: Kathy Middleton
Photo research: James Nixon
Editors: Paul Humphrey, James Nixon, Rachel Eagen
Proofreader: Wendy Scavuzzo
Layout: sprout.uk.com
Illustrations: sprout.uk.com
Cover design and logo: Margaret Amy Salter
Production coordinator and prepress
    technician: Tammy McGarr
Print coordinator: Margaret Amy Salter

Produced for Crabtree Publishing Company by
Discovery Books

Photographs:
Alamy: pp. 21 top (Caro), 21 bottom (H. Mark Weidman
    Photography), 22 (Tony Hertz), 28 (Claudia
    Hechtenberg/Caro), 29 top (varioimagesGmbH &
    Co.KG).
Corbis: pp. 10 top (Philip Evans/Visuals Unilimited), 16
    (cultura), 18 (Hybrid Images/cultura), 27 (Laguna
    Design/Science Photo Library).
Getty Images: pp. 15 bottom (Robert W. Kelley/Time &
    Life Pictures), 26 (Bloomberg).
NuVision Engineering Inc, Mooresville, NC USA: p. 20.
Shutterstock: cover (except background and eye
    dropper), pp. 4 (Photo Smile), 5 (Rgtimeline), 7 bottom
    (branislavpudar), 8 top (Vasilyev), 8 middle (Aaron
    Amat), 9 top (snapgalleria), 9 bottom (zhu difeng), 10
    bottom (Andreas G. Karelias), 11 bottom-right
    (michaeljung), 12 top (somchai rakin), 14 (Tyler Olson),
    17 top (Marcin Balcerzak), 17 bottom (Sirikorn
    Techatraibhop), 19 top (Andresr), 23 top (Rgtimeline),
    23 bottom (B. Brown), 24 (Darla Hallmark), 29 bottom
    (Christian Lagerek).
Thinkstock: cover (background and eye dropper).
Wikimedia: pp. 6 (Hermann Ost), 7 top (William Barclay
    Parsons Collection/New York Public Library
    Archives), 8 bottom (National Portrait Gallery), 12
    bottom (Yuri Raysper), 13 (Robin Muller), 19 bottom
    (Tinkering Bell), 25 (Wikiphoto).

Library and Archives Canada Cataloguing in Publication

Snedden, Robert, author
    Chemical engineering and chain reactions / Robert Snedden.

(Engineering in action)
Includes index.
Issued in print and electronic formats.
ISBN 978-0-7787-1197-1 (bound).--ISBN 978-0-7787-1230-5 (pbk.)
ISBN 978-1-4271-8948-6 (pdf).--ISBN 978-1-4271-8944-8 (html)

    1. Chemical engineering--Juvenile literature. 2. Chemistry--
Juvenile literature. I. Title. II. Series: Engineering in action (St.
Catharines, Ont.)

TP155.S64 2013   j660   C2013-906145-2
                                      C2013-906146-0

Library of Congress Cataloging-in-Publication Data

Snedden, Robert.
 Chemical engineering and chain reactions / Robert Snedden.
    pages cm -- (Engineering in action)
 Audience: Ages 10-13.
 Audience: Grades 4 to 6.
 Includes index.
 ISBN 978-0-7787-1197-1 (reinforced library binding) -- ISBN
 978-0-7787-1230-5 (pbk.) -- ISBN 978-1-4271-8948-6 (electronic pdf) --
 ISBN 978-1-4271-8944-8 (electronic html)
 1. Chemical engineering--Juvenile literature. 2. Chemical
 processes--Juvenile literature. I. Title.

 TP147.S64 2014
 660--dc23
                                      2013035440

Crabtree Publishing Company

Printed in Canada/102013/BF20130920

www.crabtreebooks.com   1-800-387-7650

Copyright © **2014 CRABTREE PUBLISHING COMPANY**. All rights reserved. No part of this publication may be reproduced,
stored in a retrieval system or be transmitted in any form or by any means, electronic, mechanical, photocopying, recording, or other-
wise, without the prior written permission of Crabtree Publishing Company.

Published in Canada
Crabtree Publishing
616 Welland Ave.
St. Catharines, ON
L2M 5V6

Published in the United States
Crabtree Publishing
PMB 59051
350 Fifth Avenue, 59th Floor
New York, New York 10118

Published in the United Kingdom
Crabtree Publishing
Maritime House
Basin Road North, Hove
BN41 1WR

Published in Australia
Crabtree Publishing
3 Charles Street
Coburg North
VIC, 3058

CONTENTS

MATERIAL WORLD

Materials are substances from which we can make things. Some materials, such as stone and wood, need little more than cutting into shape to be useful. Other materials, such as plastics, metals, and **ceramics**, have to be obtained from **raw materials** before they can be used.

Materials technology: Chemical engineers design and build the factories that make the products we need. The food we eat, the energy we use, the medicines we take, and the clothes we wear, all depend on chemical engineering. Chemical engineers use their knowledge of physics to predict how materials will behave under different conditions. Their knowledge of chemistry tells them how different materials will **react** with each other, and what new materials will be produced by that reaction.

Chemical engineers use their knowledge to change raw materials into useful ones. From the soap you use to wash your face to the materials that make up your cell phone—chemical engineers help shape the world we live in.

Chemists and chemical engineers

Both chemists and chemical engineers deal with chemistry—the science of **matter** and the ways it can be changed. So what's the difference between the two?

Chemical engineers design and build complex oil and gas plants such as this.

Chemists most often work in laboratories with small amounts of materials. Here they will develop substances, such as food preservatives or lifesaving drugs.

Learning to be a chemical engineer starts with studying chemical reactions in the laboratory.

Chemical engineers operate on a large scale, taking the reactions that chemists have discovered and making them work in the real world rather than in laboratories. While the chemist measures materials in grams or ounces, the chemical engineer may measure them in tons. Rather than using laboratory test tubes, the chemical engineer is responsible for designing and operating industrial plants with huge steel containers and miles of piping.

Chemical solutions: Just like other engineers, chemical engineers follow an eight-step process (see below) when they are trying to design a solution to a problem. For example, a chemist may have discovered a new artificial fabric, and the chemical engineer's job is to work out how to produce enough to start making clothes from it.

EARLY ENGINEERING

The simple art of bread making can be thought of as chemical engineering. Yeast is used to change the **starch** in flour into a gas called **carbon dioxide**, which makes the bread rise. The technique was first discovered by the Egyptians about 6,000 years ago.

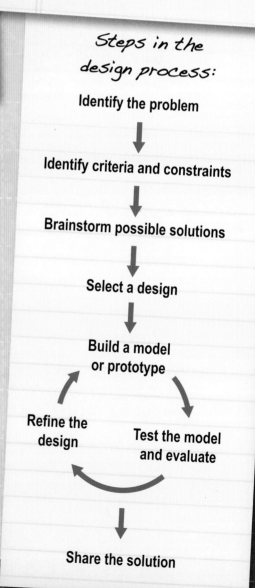

Steps in the design process:

Identify the problem

↓

Identify criteria and constraints

↓

Brainstorm possible solutions

↓

Select a design

↓

Build a model or prototype

Test the model and evaluate

Refine the design

↓

Share the solution

ENGINEERING PIONEERS

The beginnings of modern chemical engineering can be seen in the **Industrial Revolution** that swept through Europe, North America, and the rest of the world in the 18th and 19th centuries.

Production process: Nicolas Leblanc was born in 1742 near Orleans, France. He was wealthy enough to have his own laboratory, where he developed his interest in chemistry. In 1783, Leblanc set out to meet a challenge set by the French Academy of Sciences to develop a cheap way to produce large amounts of sodium carbonate. This is an important chemical in the manufacture of glass, soap, and paper.

*The process Leblanc developed involved heating sea salt with a chemical called sulfuric acid. It was very successful in producing sodium carbonate. However, it also produced poisonous chemicals that killed trees for miles around. This was one of the first examples of industrial **pollution**. Despite this hazard, Leblanc's process was widely used and became an important part of Europe's growing chemical industry.*

Part of the process Leblanc designed involved heating chemicals in a rotating furnace.

Before the Industrial Revolution, chemicals were produced on a small scale in laboratories. But the new industries needed chemicals in larger quantities. For example, sulfuric acid was used in the manufacture of **detergents** and **fertilizers**, and to remove rust from iron and steel. Calcium hypochlorite (bleaching powder) cut down the time it took to produce textiles, which previously were bleached by the sun.

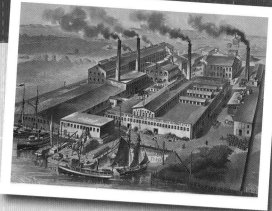

The early factories producing fertilizers and other chemicals often caused a great deal of pollution.

THE FATHER OF CHEMICAL ENGINEERING

The term "chemical engineer" was in general use by about 1900, largely as a result of the work of British engineer George E. Davis (1850-1906). Davis is regarded as the father of modern chemical engineering. He identified a number of features that all chemical factories had in common, such as the need to transport and process materials. He wrote a book based on his findings called A Handbook of Chemical Engineering, the first manual of its kind.

Chemical engineers produce chemicals, such as these detergents, and the plastic containers that hold them.

STATES OF MATTER

Matter is all around us. Everything we can see, touch, smell, and feel is made up of matter—including us! Matter is formed from tiny particles called **atoms**.

Atoms and molecules

Atoms link together to form molecules. Molecules made up of just one kind of atom are called **elements**. For example, two oxygen atoms join together to make an oxygen molecule. A compound is made up of different kinds of atoms linked together. For example the sodium chloride, or common salt, molecule is formed from atoms of sodium and chlorine. The water molecule is a combination of oxygen and hydrogen atoms.

Atoms of sodium (purple) link with atoms of chlorine (yellow) to form crystals of common salt (sodium chloride).

HUMPHRY DAVY

Englishman Humphry Davy (1778-1829) was one of the greatest chemists of the Industrial Revolution. He was a pioneer in the technique of using electricity to split up compounds. In the course of experiments, he discovered the elements potassium, sodium, barium, calcium, and magnesium, and showed that water could be split into hydrogen and oxygen.

Solids, liquids, and gases: Matter comes in one of three basic forms—solid, liquid, or gas. These are the three states of matter. Water is a good example of a material that can be found in all three states—as solid ice, as liquid running water, and as steam, which is water in the form of a gas.

Most substances can be changed from one state into another. If you cool the oxygen in the air we breathe to below –297°F (–183°C), it will change from a gas into a liquid. If you heat solid copper metal to 1985°F (1085°C), it melts into a liquid.

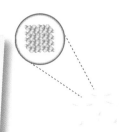
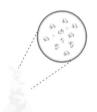

The molecules in solid ice are packed closely together (1); in liquid water, they can move around (2); and in a gas (steam), they are not joined to each other and move around freely (3).

Engineering matters

States of matter are vitally important to chemical engineers. For example, substances in the form of gases and liquids will react together much more rapidly than solids. A chemical that flows smoothly through a pipe as a liquid would clog it up if the liquid was allowed to cool and become solid.

Very high temperatures are used to **extract** metals from rock ores.

SMELTING

Smelting is a way of obtaining metals by heating rocks, called **ores**, to a high enough temperature for liquid metal to appear. The first metals to be obtained in this way were tin and lead, over 8,500 years ago. The person who discovered this technique is not known, but they were early ancestors of today's chemical engineers.

9

CHEMICAL REACTIONS

All of the different types of elements and compounds that exist are called chemicals. Each chemical has different **properties**. These affect how it behaves, or reacts, when it comes into contact with other chemicals. For example, the element potassium, a type of metal, is so highly reactive that it will burst into flame on contact with water.

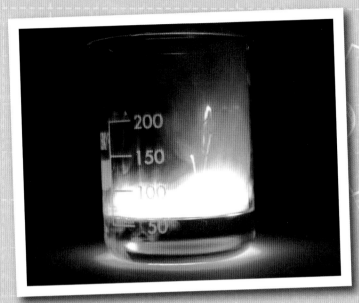

As can be seen here, potassium ignites on contact with water.

Chemical reactions are going on all around you all the time. When you put detergent in the washing machine, chemical reactions break up the dirt on your clothes. When you ride your bike, chemical reactions in your muscles produce the energy to get you moving. When the apple you forgot in the fruit bowl starts rotting, that's chemical reactions happening again.

Something new
A chemical reaction takes place when two or more chemicals react together to form new substances. For example, metals and **acids** react together to produce hydrogen gas. Chemical reactions are different from the changes that take place when a substance changes from one state of matter to another. The molecules that make up a chemical do not change when it melts or freezes.

Some chemical reactions, such as natural gas combining with oxygen on a kitchen stove, produce a lot of energy.

Chemical equations:

New molecules are formed when a chemical reaction takes place, but the total number of atoms stays the same. Chemists use chemical **equations** to set out what happens in a reaction. For instance:

$$CH_4 + 2O_2 \rightarrow CO_2 + 2H_2O$$

This is the equation for burning methane gas—the main component of natural gas, which you might use for heating or cooking in your home. If you look at the illustration, you can see that the atoms don't change but they have been rearranged into different combinations. This is what happens in a chemical reaction.

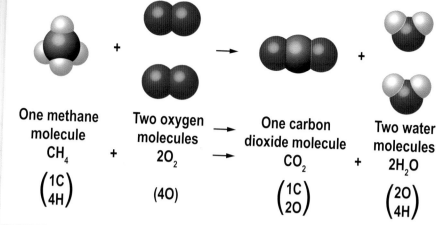

| One methane molecule CH_4 $\begin{pmatrix} 1C \\ 4H \end{pmatrix}$ | + | Two oxygen molecules $2O_2$ (4O) | One carbon dioxide molecule CO_2 $\begin{pmatrix} 1C \\ 2O \end{pmatrix}$ | + | Two water molecules $2H_2O$ $\begin{pmatrix} 2O \\ 4H \end{pmatrix}$ |

When methane combines with oxygen, a chemical reaction takes place that produces carbon dioxide gas and water. No new atoms are formed and none are lost, so there is an equal number on each side of the equation.

Reactants and products

The substances that take part in chemical reactions are called reactants, and the substances produced by the reaction are called products. Chemical engineers have to know how different substances will react with each other and what products will be formed.

It is important for the chemical engineer to know the proportions of each reactant involved in a reaction. This allows them to measure the exact amounts of each substance needed so there is no waste of materials. Figuring out how to balance chemical equations allows them to do that.

In the laboratory, the correct amounts of each chemical are carefully measured out.

REACTION ENGINEERING

Some chemical reactions take place much more rapidly than others. Controlling the rate of a chemical reaction is a major part of what chemical engineers do.

Chemical kinetics

The study of the rate of chemical reactions is called chemical kinetics. Kinetic means moving, so kinetic energy is the energy of movement. For chemical reactions to take place, the molecules taking part in the reaction have to be on the move, so they can come into contact with each other. If the molecules come together with enough force, they will break up and reform into new compounds.

Chemical engineers use machines like this stirring device to make sure chemicals are properly mixed together and will react with each other.

Reaction rates: It is very important for the chemical engineer to know how easily chemicals will react with each other. Chemical reactions can be slow, such as the change that takes place when iron combines with oxygen to form iron oxide, or rust (above). They can also be very rapid. Combustion, or burning, is the rapid combination of oxygen with a fuel. Methane gas combines with oxygen as it burns to produce carbon dioxide and water, as well as a lot of heat and light energy.

Rate changes

There are various ways that the rate of chemical reaction can be changed. Increasing pressure squeezes the molecules in a gas into a smaller space, increasing the chances of collisions. Heating the chemicals involved in a reaction gives the molecules more kinetic energy. They move around faster and are more likely to collide with each other. Cooling the chemicals makes the molecules slower. Freezing food stops it from going bad by slowing down the reactions that cause it to rot.

It is difficult to get a sugar cube (left) to burn, but chemicals found in ash act as catalysts, making it burn more readily if ash is rubbed on to the cube (right).

Catalysts: Catalysts are one of the chemical engineer's most important tools. A catalyst is a chemical that can change the rate of a chemical reaction without being changed itself. Catalysts are used in a number of manufacturing processes such as making plastics and fertilizers. For example, one of the steps in producing nitric acid, an important chemical in fertilizer production, is heating ammonia (see page 14) with oxygen in the presence of a platinum (a type of metal) catalyst. Chemical engineers can add substances called promoters that increase the activity of a catalyst. Other substances, called inhibitors or poisons, can reduce the catalyst's effects.

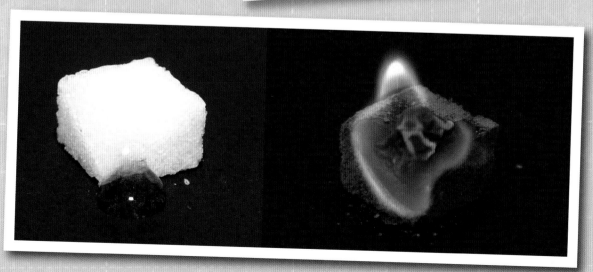

FROM IDEA TO INDUSTRY

Chemical engineers have to understand how materials work on the very smallest scales—that of atoms and molecules. But they also have to know how the reactions that take place in the laboratory can be scaled up to work at an industrial level.

The vast wheat fields that provide so many of us with food need huge amounts of fertilizer.

The Haber-Bosch Process: The Haber-Bosch process for making ammonia gas is one of the most important in the history of chemical engineering, and a good example of how chemists and chemical engineers work together.

To grow properly crops need fertilizers that contain nitrogen. Most of the air that surrounds us is made up of nitrogen gas, but it has to form part of a compound before plants can use it. Scientists began to look for ways to produce a compound that could be used in fertilizers.

In his laboratory in Germany in 1908, chemist Fritz Haber found a way to combine nitrogen from the air with hydrogen to make the compound ammonia. The equipment he developed used high temperatures and pressures, and an iron catalyst, and could produce a cupful of ammonia in two hours. Today, more than 100 million tons of ammonia are used each year to fertilize crops around the world.

Setting up production

If Haber's process was to have a practical benefit, it would obviously have to be carried out on a much larger scale. Chemical engineer Carl Bosch took on the task. He faced many problems in setting up Haber's process in a factory. Thousands of experiments were carried out to find the best catalyst to use. Eventually, Bosch and his team found that iron with a small amount of aluminum was the most effective solution.

New types of steel that could cope with the high pressures had to be developed and tested. Containers and pipes were encased in reinforced concrete, yet they still burst. Bosch finally managed to design a double pipe strong enough for the task and, in 1913, the first ammonia factory went into production.

The Haber-Bosch process

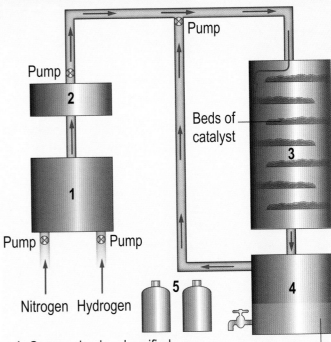

Pump

Pump

2

Beds of catalyst

3

1

Pump

Pump

Nitrogen   Hydrogen

5

4

Liquid ammonia

1. Gases mixed and purified
2. Gases compressed (squeezed)
3. Gases heated to 840°F (449°C)
4. The ammonia produced is separated from leftover gases in cooler
5. Ammonia storage tanks

THE MOST IMPORTANT SCIENTIFIC DISCOVERY

Professor Vaclav Smil of the University of Manitoba believes that the Haber-Bosch process is "the most important scientific discovery." Without it, around three billion of the world's population would not be alive today because we could not produce enough food for them.

Producing chemicals for fertilizers meant chemical engineers had to build huge ammonia factories like this.

DOING IT BETTER

Engineers are always looking for ways to improve how things work. Chemical engineers want to make chemical production processes as **efficient** and as cheap to run as possible.

Identify the problem: The first step in any engineering project is to identify exactly what the problem is. Before searching for solutions, the engineers will first be very clear about what it is they are trying to achieve.

For example, the smooth flow of materials from one part of a chemical plant to another is vitally important. Suppose one of the materials used was a thick, sluggish liquid. What could be done to make it move more easily through the pipes?

Criteria and constraints: In solving any problem, there are always certain conditions that have to be met. Criteria are the requirements the engineers have to meet in designing their solution. This could involve controlling how fast chemicals flow through the system and finding a way to separate the product they are making from any waste materials. Constraints are the limits placed on the design by things such as the location of the factory, the materials that can be used, the cost involved, and possible effects on the environment.

Chemical engineers carefully check the test results on a laptop as they discuss ways of improving the factory.

SAFETY FIRST

One of the major constraints on any chemical engineering project is safety. Chemical engineers are trained to look very carefully at the safety aspects of their designs. Many of the substances used in chemical engineering processes are toxic, **corrosive**, or even explosive, so their safe handling is vital.

Many chemicals can be very hazardous, so it is important for chemical engineers to wear protective clothing when handling them.

A BETTER BATTERY

Portable electronics, such as cell phones, mp3 players, and tablet computers, play a large role in our everyday lives. But without a source of power, these gadgets are useless. The answer came thanks to Japanese chemical engineer Yoshio Nishi, who led the team that designed the high-power, rechargeable batteries used by our high-tech devices.

Lithium is a highly reactive metal and can easily catch fire. In the early stages of development, there were many who thought lithium was much too dangerous a chemical to be used in batteries. However, lithium batteries can produce a lot of energy for their size. Nishi and his team were able to solve the problem of making the batteries safe.

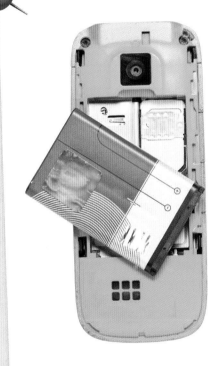

The team came up with a variety of design solutions. These included a safe way to store the lithium in the battery and a device that would prevent the battery from working if it overheated. The work was not easy. Nishi said that the team "experienced one difficulty after another." With the solutions in place, lithium batteries went into production in 1991 and are now widely used in mobile devices.

We wouldn't be able to use mobile devices without the invention of lightweight, rechargeable batteries to power them.

SEARCHING FOR SOLUTIONS

Once they are sure what the problem is, and the criteria and constraints have been considered, the engineers begin the next step in the problem-solving process—the search for a practical solution.

Brainstorming: One of the first things the engineering team will do is to share ideas with each other in a **brainstorming** session. In a good brainstorming session, ideas are allowed to flow from everyone. Every idea will be listened to without being criticized or rejected. Even those that might sound ridiculous at first could turn out to be the key to solving the problem.

Designing the best: The best ideas from the brainstorming session will be worked up into designs and **blueprints**. The engineers looking for a way to make a sluggish liquid flow faster might decide that the best solution would be to heat it. They will sketch designs for the chemical plant that include heated storage tanks and pipes.

A team of chemical engineers will carefully examine a problem, then discuss the best way to solve it.

These days we find sticky notes everywhere—but it took a chemical engineer to find a way to produce them.

AN INVENTION AND AN IDEA

In 1968, American chemist Spencer Silver found a way to make a glue that was strong enough to stick one piece of paper to another, but weak enough to allow them to be pulled apart without damage. Silver thought his unique glue had potential, but he wasn't sure what do with it. No one could come up with an idea to turn his discovery into a product that could be sold.

An American chemical engineer called Arthur Fry eventually heard about Silver's glue and had an idea. He thought it would be perfect for sticky, but removable, bookmarks. He sent a file to one of his colleagues, using one of his sticky bookmarks to indicate something interesting. His colleague sent the file back, having used the bookmark to scribble a note to Fry. Fry realized he didn't just have a bookmark—he had sticky notes! The next step was to produce the sticky notes in bulk.

When Fry couldn't find a machine that could manufacture his sticky notes in bulk, he built one of his own in his basement and started production. Post-It Notes, as they came to be called, went on sale to the public in 1980 12 years after Silver's discovery and have been a success ever since.

Arthur Fry, the inventor of the Post-It Note.

TESTING TIMES

It's not enough for an idea to look good on paper. The next step is to make a working model of the chemical production process.

Prototypes: To find out if their idea will work, the engineers will build and test a prototype. A prototype is a first working model of the engineering process they plan to put into operation. The engineers will look very carefully for flaws in this prototype. If it doesn't perform to their expectations, the engineers will go "back to the drawing board" to look for a different solution, then build another model to test. The engineers may have to try out several different designs to find the one that works best.

Computer modeling

Heating a thick liquid to make it flow more easily may be too expensive or too dangerous, so engineers might look at other ideas such as forcing the liquid through the pipes at high pressure. In the early stages of the design process, engineers may try out ideas by running them on computer programs. This allows them to see what might happen in the

Prototypes such as this chemical cleaning tank can be tested before being installed in factories.

process if, for example, they raise the temperature or pressure. A tool that has become available to engineers in recent years is the 3D printer. This can turn computer designs into plastic models so that prototypes may be assembled quickly and easily.

Testing to destruction

Engineers may deliberately push their models to extremes to make them fail, for safety reasons. This is called testing to destruction. It tells the engineers how to make sure the equipment is used safely when they come to install it in a factory. It is much better that a pipe cracks under high pressure in a carefully controlled test in the engineering laboratory than to have it happen unexpectedly where people are working.

A chemical engineer tries out a new process on a small scale in a laboratory. If it is successful, a full-size version can be used in a factory.

Chemical engineers test their products to destruction. This engineer is testing what will happen if a product catches fire.

Design improvements: Using all they have learned from testing their prototypes, the engineers will work on their design, making improvements to it until they are happy with the results. Satisfied that they have the best possible solution to their problem, the engineers will be ready to go into full-scale production.

INTO PRODUCTION

Building a chemical production plant is a costly and complicated process and chemical engineers will work closely with mechanical engineers, civil engineers, and environmental engineers to ensure that everything works safely and efficiently.

The chemical industry uses many hazardous materials and can produce a lot of waste. Because of this, chemical and environmental engineers work together to ensure that pollution is kept to a minimum and that the waste products of the chemical processing can be recycled or disposed of safely.

Where to build: The choice of where to build a chemical plant is as important as the actual design of the plant. The raw materials needed for chemical processing should be readily available, and there has to be a way of transporting the finished products to where they are needed.

Chemical plants are usually built a safe distance from housing to protect people from the waste that is produced.

In 2013, Shell Chemicals were trying to decide whether to build a plastics manufacturing plant in western Pennsylvania. Supplies of natural gas in the area would be used as the raw materials for the process. A spokesperson for the company outlined some of the things that had to be considered: "There are many hurdles to clear... We need to...secure supply [of materials], complete the engineering and design work, confirm the support of customers for our products...and complete a thorough environmental and technical review of the location before we can confirm its suitability."

A technician inspects the pills in a drug manufacturing plant to ensure they are of a high quality.

Engineers had to design and build this machine which automatically counts out the right number of pills into each bottle.

FROM TEST BENCH TO PHARMACY

The drug manufacturing industry produces thousands of different medicines that are used to treat different kinds of illnesses. Before a drug is approved for use, it has to go through a series of rigorous tests to prove that it is effective and safe. These tests can take years but, after they are done, it is time to start the manufacturing process. This is where the chemical engineers come in.

The engineers will look at the costs involved and at the best production methods for manufacturing the drug. They will work with the chemists who developed the drug to adapt the process carried out in the laboratory to one that can be used for mass production in a factory. Milling machines will be used to pound chemicals into fine particles and mixing machines will combine them together in exactly the right amounts. Then the ingredients will be mixed into solutions, pressed into pills or enclosed in capsules. Finally the drugs will be packaged up ready to be transported to hospitals and pharmacies.

DESIGN CHALLENGE: MAKE A FIRE EXTINGUISHER

A fire needs two things—a source of fuel, and oxygen, which it gets from the air. A fire extinguisher works by cutting the fire off from its source of oxygen. A common type of household fire extinguisher smothers the fire with carbon dioxide gas. In this project, you will make a carbon dioxide fire extinguisher that can put out a small candle flame. Be sure to ask an adult to supervise.

1: The problem: How can you stop oxygen from reaching a candle flame?

2: Criteria and constraints: The fire extinguisher has to be safe to use and made from things you might find around the house. It must produce carbon dioxide and you must be able to direct it to where it is needed.

3: Brainstorm solutions: We need to know how different chemicals work together. If you add baking soda to vinegar, they react and produce lots of carbon dioxide. How can you make use of this to put out the candle flame? You'll need something to hold your chemicals, and a way to direct the carbon dioxide toward the flame.

Carbon dioxide fire extinguishers are commonly used to smother fires by cutting the fire off from a supply of oxygen.

4: Decide on your design: Try to put all of your ideas together in a design. As you sketch your designs, make a note of any equipment you will need. Once you have decided which design you think will work best, you can make a prototype.

5: Make a prototype: A prototype will let you test your design. Perhaps your idea is something like this: A bottle to hold the vinegar and baking soda; a cork made of modeling clay to fit the neck of the bottle; and a bendy straw through the middle of the clay to allow the carbon dioxide to escape and to use as a way to direct it toward the flame.

6: Test the prototype: Ask an adult to set up the candle safely and light it for you. Fill the bottle about a third full with vinegar then add a tablespoon of baking soda. Plug the bottle with the modeling clay and straw and give it a shake to get it fizzing! Tilt the bottle carefully to get carbon dioxide flowing through the straw. Use the straw to direct the carbon dioxide toward the candle. Don't let the candle flame touch the straw!

You will need a suitable container for your chemicals.

7: Make improvements: Did the flame go out? Did it go out fairly quickly or did it take a while? Do you get more fizz if you add vinegar to the baking soda instead of the other way around? Is the straw wide enough to let enough carbon dioxide escape? Each time you make changes to your prototype, try it again to find out if it works better.

8: Communicate: Engineers work together on their ideas. Let other people see your model fire extinguisher in action. Ask them what ideas they might have to make it work better.

FUTURE TRENDS

What might chemical engineers be involved with in the future? Biochemistry (the chemistry that happens in living things) and biotechnology (using biological processes for industrial purposes), the development of new drugs, improved fertilizers and **pesticides**, and the search for new sources of energy can all benefit from input from chemical engineers.

Environmental issues

Chemical engineers are a vital part of the teams of scientists and engineers that are tackling the problems of pollution and **global warming.** The exhaust from cars and other vehicles is a major source of air pollution. Chemical engineers have helped reduce the amount of pollution produced by gas-burning engines by finding ways to produce fuels that burn cleaner. They are also designing engines that use less fuel and devices that use catalysts to break down the pollutants found in exhaust pipes.

Hydrogen is a very clean fuel. Hydrogen **fuel cells** produce electricity directly from hydrogen and oxygen, and the only waste product they produce is water. Vehicles running on fuel cells would emit none of the pollutants associated with today's vehicles. But there are problems to be solved before they can be widely used. Chemical engineers are working to develop safe ways to produce enough hydrogen from **fossil fuels** cheaply, or by splitting water into hydrogen and oxygen.

Engineers carry out a demonstration of a model fuel cell. They hope to be able to make full-size versions that will power vehicles.

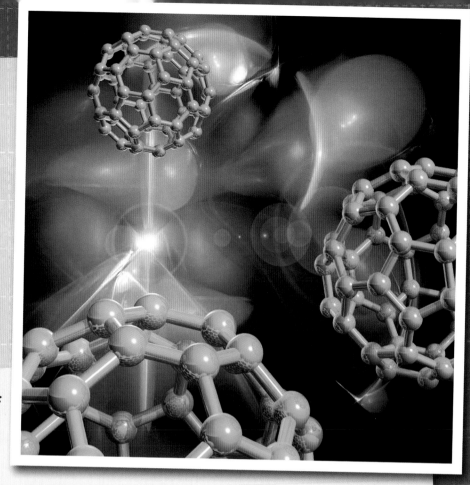

Scientists and engineers are still investigating possible uses for these tiny balls of carbon atoms called fullerenes.

Advances in medicine: A fantastic amount of chemistry goes on in the human body. Chemical engineers can use their knowledge to help medical researchers come up with new ways to treat injury and illness.

Fullerenes are a recently discovered form of carbon. They can form into microscopically small, hollow balls of just 60 carbon atoms. Chemical engineers are developing ways of taking them from the laboratory test tube to full-scale production. Due to their small size, fullerenes could be an excellent way of delivering precise quantities of a drug to exactly where it is needed within the body. Researchers are also investigating using fullerenes to carry tiny amounts of radioactive materials (materials that give off energy) to the sites of **cancer cells** in the body. This would allow doctors to attack the cancer cells but leave surrounding healthy cells unharmed.

SO YOU WANT TO BE A CHEMICAL ENGINEER?

What skills do you need to be a chemical engineer? What are the typical activities a chemical engineer is likely to be involved in on a day-to-day basis? What is it like to actually be a chemical engineer?

If you want to be a chemical engineer, you should enjoy finding creative solutions to problems and working with other people. You definitely need to study chemistry and math at school. Another science subject, such as physics, would be helpful too.

A chemical engineering student gets hands-on experience at working in a chemical plant.

The life of an engineer: Marcella Goodnight is a chemical engineer with a large research company in California, where she is working on ways of producing chemicals to be used in the manufacture of medicines. She decided on chemical engineering as a career after following advice from her chemistry teacher who recognized her talent for chemistry, physics, and math. She finds a lot about her job that's rewarding. "I'm getting paid to do something that I like. I really like designing the process equipment—I love tinkering with these big toys. Every time I get equipment, in I'm just like a little kid at Christmas. I can't wait to open it and start testing it. My typical day involves coordination with other groups to see what equipment they're going to be using... to find out what they can support us on, and to make sure that we have the utilities [equipment] that we're going to require."

Career opportunities

As a chemical engineer, you would have many different career choices. The success of many industries is dependent on chemical engineering. Manufacturing paper, pharmaceuticals, metals, and plastics, all depend on chemical processes. The **nuclear power** industry relies on chemical engineering for manufacturing fuels and the reprocessing of wastes. Food, cosmetics, and textiles production all make use of the chemical engineer's expertise.

The oil industry is a major employer of chemical engineers. They look for the most effective ways of getting oil and natural gas from beneath the ground or the sea. They help to develop better ways of locating new oil and gas deposits. They improve the running of oil **refineries** to make them as efficient as possible. They search for safer and more efficient methods of developing oil-based products such as plastics. Without chemical engineers, there would be no oil industry.

Producing everyday products such as skin cream is just one of the many things chemical engineers do for us.

A chemical engineer checks a pipeline inside an oil refinery.

LEARNING MORE

BOOKS

Tom Adams, *Molecule Mayhem*, Templar Publishing, 2012

Emma Carlson Berne, *Transforming! Chemical Energy*, PowerKids Press, 2013

Jay Hawkins, *Material World: The Science of Matter*, Windmill Books, 2013

Will Hurd, *Changing States: Solids, Liquids, and Gases*, Heinemann Library, 2009

Tom Jackson, *Introducing the Periodic Table (Why Chemistry Matters)*, Crabtree Publishing, 2012

Rebecca W. Keller, Ph.D., *21 Super Simple Chemistry Experiments*, Gravitas Publications Inc, 2012

ONLINE

www.ceb.cam.ac.uk/exemplarch2002/mcp21/index.html
What is Chemical Engineering? Find the answer here.

www.chemicalengineering.org
Discover the many ways chemical engineers are changing the world, now and in the future.

http://chenected.aiche.org
A site created for chemical engineers but everyone can enjoy it.

www.discoverengineering.org
Learn about all aspects of engineering— including chemical engineering.

http://kidsahead.com/subjects/21-other-stem-subjects/cool_jobs/194
An interview with a real-life chemical engineer!

http://engineeryourlife.org/cms/Careers/Descriptions/2961.aspx
Find out what's involved in becoming a chemical engineer.

PLACES TO VISIT

The Chemical Heritage Foundation Museum, Philadelphia: www.chemheritage.org

Canada Science and Technology Museum, Ottawa: www.sciencetech.technomuses.ca

GLOSSARY

acids Corrosive substances that can dissolve metals

atoms The tiny particles of matter from which all materials are made

blueprints Engineering designs, usually done as white lines on a blue background

brainstorming Finding answers to problems by sharing ideas among a group of people

cancer cells Damaged cells in the body that divide, spread to other parts of the body, and can cause death

carbon dioxide A colorless and odorless gas that animals breathe out through their lungs; is also formed when any fuel containing carbon is burned; carbon is a common element that is present in many compounds

ceramics Pieces of clay that have been hardened by heat

corrosive Describes a substance that will damage or destroy other substances it comes into contact with; acids are examples of corrosive substances

detergents Chemical cleaning agents that combine with dirt and grease to make them dissolve more easily in water

efficient To do something in a way that gives the maximum results with the minimum of wasted effort

elements Substances that cannot be broken down into simpler substances by chemical reactions; an element is made up of just one type of atom

equations Sequences of symbols that represent the changes that happen in chemical reactions

extract To remove or obtain something from a substance

fertilizers Substances added to soil to help plants grow

fossil fuels Fuels that formed from the ancient remains of plants and animals that lived millions of years ago; coal, petroleum, and natural gas are fossil fuels

fuel cells Devices similar to batteries that convert chemical energy into electrical energy using hydrogen as a fuel

global warming A rise in the average temperature of Earth, believed by most scientists to result from rising levels of gases in the atmosphere that trap heat

Industrial Revolution The shift toward large-scale factory production that took place in the 18th and 19th centuries

matter The physical substance from which all objects are formed

nuclear power Power generated by releasing the energy stored in atoms

ores Minerals that contain valuable metal that can be extracted

pesticides Substances used to destroy insects and other animals that may cause damage to crops

pollution Something that adds harmful substances to the air, water, or soil

properties A property is a quality or characteristic of something; for example, one of the properties of metals is that they conduct electricity

raw materials The basic materials used in the manufacture of something

react To take part in a reaction, a chemical process that changes one set of chemical substances into a different set of substances

refineries Factories where unwanted substances are removed

starch A white, tasteless powder that is found in foods, such as rice, breads, and potatoes

INDEX